Wood

Claire Llewellyn

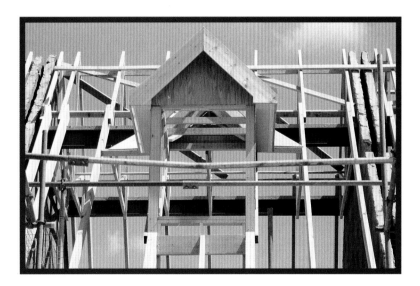

FRANKLIN WATTS

LONDON•SYDNEY

First published in 2004
by Franklin Watts
96 Leonard Street
London EC2A 4XD

Franklin Watts Australia
45-51 Huntley Street
Alexandria, NSW 2015

Text copyright © Claire Llewellyn 2004
Design and concept © Franklin Watts 2004

Series advisor: Gill Matthews, non-fiction literacy
consultant and Inset trainer
Editor: Rachel Cooke
Series design: Peter Scoulding
Designer: James Marks
Photography: Ray Moller unless otherwise credited
Acknowledgements: T. Bognar/Art Directors/Trip:11l, 22br. I.Burgandinov/Art Directors/Trip: 17.
Sarah Errington/Hutchison: 12. Image Works/Topham: 7, 13. Jack Kurtz/Image Works/Topham: 21.
Jules Perrier/Corbis: 9tl. Helene Rogers/Art Directors/Trip: 10, 15, 23cl. Jorgen Shytte/Still Pictures: 20.
Syracuse Newspapers/Image Works/Topham: 16, 19tl. Paul Thompson/Eye Ubiquitous: 18.
Thanks to our model Jaydee Cozzi.

ISBN: 0 7496 5719 7

Printed in Malaysia

Contents

Wood is useful

Wood is a very useful material. All sorts of things are made of wood.

▼ *These things are all made of wood.*

Toy

Pencils

4

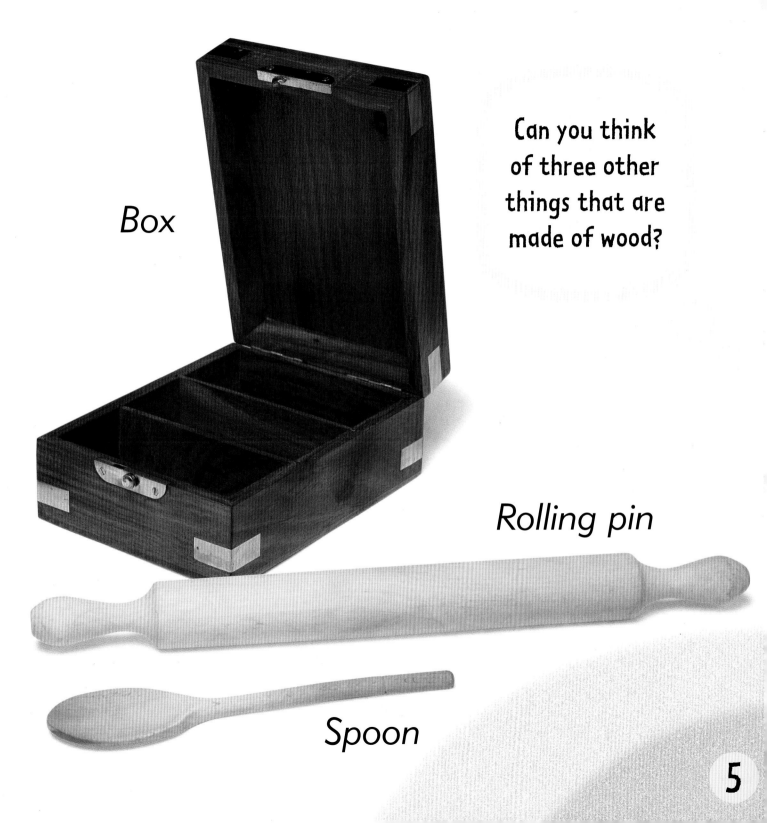

Box

Can you think of three other things that are made of wood?

Rolling pin

Spoon

5

Wood is strong

Wood is strong. It is used to build houses that will last for many years.

▶ *These wooden beams will hold up the roof.* .

Wooden stairs are very strong.

Have a look around your home. Which parts of it are made of wood?

Wood feels smooth

Wood is smooth to touch.

► *A wooden chair is smooth to sit on.*

A wooden floor is smooth to sit on.

We rub wood with polish to keep it smooth and shiny.

Take care when you rub wood. Some wood can give you splinters.

Wood floats

Wood floats in water.
Many boats are made of wood.

▲ *Wooden boats are used for fishing...*

Wood slowly rots in water. People paint or varnish wooden boats to make them waterproof.

▲ *and carrying things from place to place.*

Wood burns

Wood burns easily.
When it burns, wood gives out heat.

▲ *Firewood is used to cook food…*

▼ *and to keep people warm.*

WARNING
Fire is very
dangerous.
Never play
with fire.

Wood comes from trees

Wood comes from the trunk and branches of trees. It is a natural material.

▶ *Some trees grow in forests and woods.*

▶ *The wood is under the bark of a tree.*

Wood

Bark

Branch

Trunk

Trees take a long time to grow. It can take 50 years or more before a tree is ready to be cut down.

From tree to plank

Trees are cut into logs.
Then the logs are cut into planks.

▶*The trees are cut down with a saw. The big logs are taken to a sawmill.*

▼ *At the sawmill, the logs are cut into planks.*

We must keep planting new trees. Then we will always have plenty of wood.

How is the wood used?

When wood leaves the sawmill it is used in many ways.

▶ *Some wood goes to builders.*

Paper is made from wood. If you look closely at some kinds of paper, you can see the tiny bits of wood.

▲ *Some wood goes to paper mills. It is made into paper.*

◀ *Some wood is made into furniture.*

19

Shaping wood

Wood is easy to cut and shape.

▲ *You can make things by cutting wood and sticking it together.*

▼ *You can shape wood by carving and rubbing.*

A person who works with wood is called a carpenter.

I know that...

1 Wood is a useful material.

2 Wood is strong.

3 Wood feels smooth.

4 Wood floats.

5 Wood burns easily.

6 Wood comes from trees.

7 Trees are cut into logs and then planks.

8 Wood is used to make houses, furniture, paper and many other things.

9 Wood is easy to cut and shape.

Index

About this book

I Know That! is designed to introduce children to the process of gathering information and using reference books, one of the key skills needed to begin more formal learning at school. For this reason, each book's structure reflects the information books children will use later in their learning career – with key information in the main text and additional facts and ideas in the captions. The panels give an opportunity for further activities, ideas or discussions. The contents page and index are helpful reference guides.

The language is carefully chosen to be accessible to children just beginning to read. Illustrations support the text but also give information in their own right; active consideration and discussion of images is another key referencing skill. The main aim of the series is to build confidence – showing children how much they already know and giving them the ability to gather new information for themselves. With this in mind, the *I know that...* section at the end of the book is a simple way for children to revisit what they already know as well as what they have learnt from reading the book.